Confession can change your life

Father David M. Knight

Credits: cover, 3, 5—Paul Sequeira; 15, 34—Paul S. Conklin; 19—Religious News Service; 28, 37—Ed Lettau; 30—Edward Wallowitch.

ISBN: 0-89570-102-2

First Printing, March 1977
Second Printing, June 1979

Claretian Publications

Confession can change your life

Father David M. Knight

Introduction

EVER THINK ABOUT THE MORNING AFTER in the story of the Prodigal Son? The boy is forgiven, restored to the good graces of his father, the celebration has been held, and the fatted calf is a pleasant memory.

Then what?

To end the story with the father's forgiveness of his son is to leave out half the reality. There was a lot more to the boy's leaving than just an abstract offense against his father. A whole network of relationships with other people had been broken off or altered. A lot of confidence was shaken. People who thought they knew the boy before he left home found out that they didn't really, or that he had changed. When he came home, they weren't sure how to relate to him. There was reconciling to do.

Reconciliation means that relationships are clarified and accepted again. People explain to one another where they stand, who they really are, what their past actions should say and should not say about their present state of mind, their true orientation of heart and will. To be reconciled with another is to feel you know that person again; you know what to expect of the person, what you can count on.

There's a big difference between forgiveness and reconciliation. The church recognizes this, and is speaking of confession today more and more in terms of reconciliation. This doesn't make it any less a sacrament of forgiveness, but if we see confession as a ritual to obtain God's forgiveness only, our picture would be not only incomplete but distorted.

To see forgiveness of sin just as the act of being restored to the good graces of a previously angry God—a God who will punish us if we do not get right with Him again through sincere repentance and this religious ritual—is to understand sin and repentance, forgiveness and reconcilation in a pre-Christian way. Jesus changed all that.

Because of Jesus and his redeeming life, death, and resurrection we are in an entirely different relationship with God.

God is not for Christians the angry God the pagans knew and feared, or feared because they did not know Him. When we sin,

we do not have to win forgiveness from Him by placating his offended majesty with sacrifices or satisfying his aroused justice with penitential practices and prayers. God is our loving Father. He waits for us with anxious care before we ever turn back to Him, while we are "still a long way off." The moment He sees us coming toward Him again He is deeply moved. He runs out to meet us, throws his arms around us, and kisses us (Luke 15:20).

The prodigal son didn't even have time to tell all his sins—to make what we call an integral confession. Before he could finish the little speech of apology he had prepared, the father interrupted him, called for a robe and a ring, and told the servants

5

to bring on the fatted calf. His forgiveness was never even in question.

This is the way Jesus describes the Father. As for God the Son, He is our Savior, not our Judge (John 8:15). He is on our side. He came to earth precisely to "search out and save what was lost" (Luke 19:10). He is the good shepherd, laying down his life for the sheep (John 10:11), leaving the 99 to follow the lost one until He finds it (Luke 15:4). And when He finds it, He "puts it on his shoulders in jubilation." What He wants is to restore the sheep to the fold, not to keep it at a distance. Not to punish us for sin, but to fight for us and with us against the sin which is our common enemy.

And when we recall that the name given to the Holy Spirit—the Paraclete, or Advocate—means the same as (although much more than) lawyer, we begin to get the picture. Suppose you had prepared your defense for days with your lawyer, wondering who the judge would be, and how you could expect him to hear your case, and then found when you finally got to court, that your lawyer had been appointed as judge, while remaining at the same time your lawyer! Well, the Holy Spirit, who has been sent to us by the Father and Son to speak for us, to be at our side and counsel us, is one God with the Father and the Son. Our Judge, our Savior, and our Advocate are all one and the same!

The intention of the Gospels is to deliver us from that fear of an angry God and that worry about God's attitude toward us which weighed on pagan minds. It is not the forgiveness of God we have to be primarily concerned about once we are in Christ Jesus; it is reconciliation with our brothers.

Our great commandment is not justice, but love. We fail God most deeply as Christians when we fail to be for one another what we are gathered together to be in love.

That is why our sins—our shortfallings—cry out, not only for forgiveness from God, but for reconciliation among ourselves. Sin doesn't just create a need in the individual for forgiveness; sin creates a need in the Body of Christ itself, in the church as a whole, for reconciliation and a restoration of relationships. It is not just a matter of restoring the sinner to God's friendship, but of restoring the wholeness of the Body of Christ. Wounds have to be healed, lines of communication repaired, confidence reestablished, bonds of understanding and love strengthened, the life of the Body quickened, the work of witness carried forward. What we have taken away from the Body by our sin, we have to restore to the Body through our repentance.

This puts confession—the sacrament of reconciliation—in a whole new light. Confession is not a matter of going into a secret little closet as an enemy of God, fearful that one is under sentence of eternal death, and coming out a friend of God with a certified ticket to heaven. It is not primarily fear of God's anger and punishment that drives us to confession; it is love of the Body of Christ and concern for the community we have damaged that draw us. Does one apologize to one's closest friend out of fear? Or out of concern for the relationship that one's actions may appear to have denied?

If we accept this new understanding of ourselves, of sin, and of the real implications of repentance, then four things should change in our basic approach to confession.

> 1. We should approach confession with less concern about being forgiven, and with much more concern, a very real concern, about repairing the damage we have done to the community of believers, to the Body of Christ, and about restoring the bonds of unity, of mutual confidence, and of love that have been weakened by our conduct. And to make this real we should look to what our sins have done—and even more to what they have said—to those who are closest to us: our family, our friends, associates at work, fellow parishioners, etc.

> 2. We should be much less concerned about keeping our sins secret and much more concerned about making our repentance known. I am not suggesting public confession of sin, of course; any sin that is secret should be kept secret. But most of the sins people confess are perfectly well known to everybody who lives with them; what others do not know, quite often, is how we ourselves feel about our sins, how we judge them. Our sins say to all who know us that we don't care about some truth, some value. Repentance says that we do care. To confess our sins is to profess our faith, and this is the real point of the

sacrament. We confess sin as sin to show that we sincerely do profess the attitudes and values of Christ as true and real. To say that we were wrong —and know that we were wrong—in what we did is to say at the same time that Jesus is right, that we believe and accept the way of life He teaches.

Confession is a way of repairing the damage we have done to the community of the church, the false witness we have borne to Christ. We, who are believers and disciples of Jesus Christ, have acted in a way that is not true to his teachings. This puts Christianity—Christ himself—in a false light. So we confess that we were not expressing the truth of the church or even of our own deeper ideals in what we did. Confession is a way of re-declaring to the church, and to those who are closest to us, who we really are, what we really believe in, what we are sincerely trying to live up to. The confession of sin is a profession of return and concern: of return if we have left or broken with the community of the faithful by actions incompatible with the profession of Christ; of concern if we have only shown less concern by behavior that didn't seem to place much value on the full profession of our faith in action. In any case, the value of confession lies not in what is kept secret, but in what is made known; namely, the truth and reality of our ideals. For this reason, when the sins we have committed are public knowledge anyway, there is no value in keeping secret what we are repenting of; it would be much better if those who are closest to us, at least, might know for what we are asking God's forgiveness and theirs.

3. A third change called for in our approach to confession is that we should not let guilt feelings narrow the focus of our attention to the wrong things we have done, but rather, in the spirit of the Gospel, approach confession with a sense of responsibility for the good we ought to be doing. The aim of confession, after all, is growth, and spiritual growth is largely a matter of changing our mind about some-

thing we didn't see before. The scriptural name for this change of mind is metanoia: sometimes translated conversion, and sometimes translated as repentance. The more we understand of what we are called to be, the more we repent of what we still remain. The closer we come to the light of Christ, the more we realize how much in the darkness we have been prior to each new moment of realization. What confession is all about is seeing more clearly where we fall short and determining more decisively how we are going to live.

4. This brings us to the last thing that we should change and that is the exclusive individuality of our preparation. We are used to examining our conscience in private. But in any other area of life or activity, if we want to know where we are falling short, we ask someone else for an objective opinion. Consultation and dialogue with others is beneficial, not only to alert us to external faults or failings, but also to help us identify and call by name our deeper attitudes and motives. Why shouldn't we ask others, who live or work or deal with us, to help us pinpoint the reasons why grace does not bear the fruit it should in our daily lives?

In the pages that follow we will go more deeply into the ways a new approach to the sacrament of reconciliation can affect our use of confession. The key to what follows is the role of the Christian community (on whatever level it exists—parish, family, or friends) in helping us use confession as a means to continuous conversion of mind and heart and will. It is by each one of us converting again and again to a closer identification with the attitudes and values of Christ, and doing this with the aid and knowledge of the Christian community, that we become more and more reconciled with each other in that loving "unity which has the Spirit as its origin and peace as its binding force" (Eph. 4:3).

Why doesn't Confession seem to work anymore?

PUT YOURSELF IN THE PRIEST'S PLACE on a typical parish confession night. An anonymous male voice behind the grill intones, "Bless me, Father, it has been about a month since my last confession." You register: "Just a month—a regular—probably a pretty conscientious Catholic." The voice continues: "Since my last confession I've been impatient with my wife a few times; probably my fault. We've had some arguments. I've told lies on maybe four or five occasions: nothing big, but I know it wasn't right. I've had too much to drink on maybe two occasions. I try to watch my language, but I've slipped a few times. And I'm probably not as good a father as I should be to my children. I mean I don't spend the time with them that I ought to, and I yell at them sometimes. I guess that's about all. For these and all my sins I am heartily sorry."

If you were the priest, what would you say? A pretty routine confession. Who doesn't get impatient, cuss a little, drink a little too much at times? At least the man seems concerned about it. He needs encouragement, realization of God's love for him. So you say some positive words, suggest he say a few Hail Mary's for a penance (or if you are a little more theological as a confessor, you might suggest he do something to make up for his faults, like bringing his wife flowers some night), and you give absolution. Close the grill, next penitent.

The man goes out feeling pretty good. He is buoyed up by the priest's encouragement, reassured that God doesn't reject him. He buys flowers for his wife and is a very easy man to live with for the rest of that evening, maybe all the following day.

Then he goes back to being himself again. Sure, he goes to confession every month, sometimes more often than that. He goes because of guilt feelings. The guilt comes from the fact that he is a problem drinker. He drinks too much, objectively speaking, every night and a good part of every day. The two occasions he had in mind in his confession referred to two weekends so taken up with drinking that he could not seriously react to anything or anyone else. But all the other days of the month, with a few exceptions, he was just tight enough in the evening and just hungover enough in the morning to be for all practical purposes completely out of touch with his wife. His children only know him in two moods: the happy, party-time poppa and the headachey-hypertense disciplinarian. What he translated into his confession as impatience with his wife and yelling at his children refers in reality to a constant state of serious marital and parental incapacitation. In other words, this man is sinning in a very serious way against the obligations of his state of life. He is a lousy husband and a worse father; he makes life miserable for his wife, and he is destroying the emotional stability of his children.

The point of the story is not what the man is doing but what he is doing about it, namely nothing. The point of the story is that the picture the man paints of himself in confession does not in any sense portray the real condition of his soul or the reality of his life as a Christian husband and father. And so the priest's response to him in confession has results that are exactly the opposite of what they should be. Instead of helping the man, confession is giving him just enough emotional release from his guilt feelings to keep him from ever facing or doing anything about his real problem, his real sin. Every time the person begins to feel guilty and depressed over the kind of husband, father, and man that he is, he can go into the confessional, turn himself in for trial before a judge who is already instructed to be sympathetic with the compassion of Christ's own heart, and present the case against himself in private with the assurance that no other witnesses for the prosecution will be allowed. He knows from experience that it is a rare priest who will take up the office of inquisitor; most priests place themselves affectively on the side of the accused and try to make him feel better. So he will go out from his session of self-accusation relieved momentarily of his guilt feelings, and falsely reassured that in the eyes of God everything is all right again in his life.

In reality nothing is all right. Everything is all wrong. But he doesn't know it or isn't facing it and the priest doesn't know it either. The only ones who know it are his wife, his children, all of his close friends, his business associates, and a miscellaneous cross-section of the general public. In other words, everyone knows it except the only two people the church can rely upon sacramentally to do something about it: the priest and the penitent. And every precaution has been taken to make sure the priest will never find out anything more than the penitent tells him. And no one will ever challenge the penitent's version of the way things are because no one will ever know what the penitent's version was.

This is one of the reasons why confession is bearing so little fruit in the church, whereas in Christ's intention it was designed to bear so much fruit.

IRONICALLY, THERE IS PROBABLY NO SACRAMENT in the church more specifically designed than confession to help a person respond to the most fundamental preaching of the gospel message: "Reform your lives, for the Kingdom of God is at hand." But the tragic irony is that confession has come to be quite consistently used—in reality abused—to reassure people, in contradiction to the Gospel, that no serious reform of their lives is necessary.

How many priests could stand up and bear witness that the one thing they almost never encounter in a typical evening of hearing confessions is a genuine conversion experience on the part of anyone? (When I say almost never I do not exclude the one or perhaps two instances on a given night that make the priest feel something special has happened to really make his day). In other words, Catholics in confession are not experiencing, expressing, or even expected to be expressing, a real act of repentance, of metanoia, a real decision to change and reform something significant in their lives. Most confessions are just reiterations of the attitudes and values the penitent has always held. People slip—they fall—into sin and they confess it. There is no conversion. In most cases the fall was just that—a stumbling along the way without any real change of course and the repentance is no deeper or different than the attitude one had toward the same sin before one ever committed it or confessed it. No one is particularly proud of being impatient with his wife or kids, for example. So everyone confesses it and keeps doing it, because everyone believes this is the kind of sin no one can really avoid. It seldom occurs to Catholics that there is a cause for impatience, at least for constant or recurring impatience, and that the cause should be systematically sought out, confessed, and taken out of one's life. Catholics seldom advert to the truth that patience, peace, love, and joy are fruits of the Holy Spirit (Gal. 5:22), which means their absence points to a lack in a person's Christian life. And what is true of such a common fault as impatience is true of all other faults: where a fault exists a cause exists. And that cause—more so than the fault itself most likely—is the real matter for confession.

If a husband and wife do not have a deeply satisfying marriage, characterized by love, peace, joy, and a real growth in the spiritual life of their children, there is a cause for that. And that cause should be sought out and brought to confession. If an individual cannot shake off a deep bitterness over the changes that have taken place in the church, or an impenetrable prejudice toward persons of other races, there is a cause for that. It is a sign of something missing in the way one is living the life of grace. That cause should be discovered and repented for—and repentance means that the cause itself should be removed from one's life, at whatever cost.

In other words, confession should deal with unearthing and rooting out. In confession the axe should be laid to the roots, and every branch that is not bearing fruit should be cut out or its connection reestablished with the source of life and fruitfulness, which is the person of Jesus Christ. Confession is an act of making the crooked ways straight and the rough ways smooth for the coming-ever-nearer of Christ the Lord into the heartland of our choices, our attitudes, our values, our lives of personal response.

Confession should deal with reform—with the kind of repentance (metanoia) that realizes the real meaning of the word: conversion, a change of mind, the acceptance of a higher value, of a different attitude in faith in the light of which we begin to see that our previous conduct has been falling short of the gospel ideal. The root meaning of the word for sin in Hebrew is to miss the mark, to fall short. Sin for a Christian does not mean to do something bad; it means to fall short of the good that one should be realizing in one's life. For a person to sin against marriage in the Christian sense it is not necessary to be unfaithful to one's spouse. It is enough just not to communicate deeply with one's spouse; not to be able to pray naturally and spontaneously together with one's husband, wife, and children; not to be personally involved in, responsible for, and effective at making one's home a truly Christian environment, a milieu in which one's children can grow in deep, personal experience of God and appreciation for the faith.

This is the area confession should deal with: reform of life until one reaches a fullness of Christian living, a fullness of life in faith, in hope, and in love. But this is not what confession has dealt with in our experience, and not what we have become accustomed to expect it to deal with. Confession as we experience it deals with forgiveness, not with reform; its concern is the taking away of sin, not conversion of mind and heart. It is a car wash, not an overhaul. We use confession like a toothbrush when we should use it like a dentist's drill. We keep brushing off the surface of our lives while the interior is being eaten away with decay. We are like chronic overeaters who go on periodic diets without ever getting down to changing our basic eating habits.

How did we get this way? There are many reasons, of course. And we will look at some of those reasons in this book.

How did the first Christians see Confession?

CATHOLICS HAVE TO REMIND THEMSELVES that confession as they know it did not become a practice in the church for something like the first 900 years of Christianity. The first confessions were public and they dealt with public sins, open crimes such as murder, adultery, and apostasy from the church. Strict penances were imposed, designed to prove the sincerity of the penitent's conversion and to purify whatever evil within that had led to or resulted from the sin. The penance imposed might include fasting, going without sleep, wearing a special penitential costume in public (sackcloth and ashes, goatskin), abstaining from marital relations, or even giving up one's trade (in which case the Christian community was expected to support the penitent with almsgiving and prayers), as Father Tad Guzie explains in *What a Modern Catholic Believes About Confession* (Thomas More Press, 1974). The penance imposed might last for a period of months, or for anywhere from five to 20 years. Sometimes a man might be required to do penance for the rest of his life—to abstain from sexual relations with his wife, for example, or give up his means of livelihood forever. And absolution was not given until after the period of penance was completed, whether this meant waiting for years, or even not receiving absolution until the penitent was actually at the point of death.

We stand aghast today at the thought of such a discipline of penance. It seems almost more barbaric than Christian. But we have to understand why it seemed the normal thing to do to the people of that time.

The early Christians were very conscious that Christianity should be a total conversion of mind and heart to Christ. The grace of Baptism, the grace of Christ, was the gift of new life—a life that brought with it the power of the Holy Spirit to live on another plane of existence. The Christian was one who had died to life as it is spontaneously lived in this world, and who had been reborn to live in every respect as the Body of Jesus Christ. One did not become a Christian in the very early days without weighing and accepting the prospect of actual, physical martyrdom. And even if one was not actually killed for believing, the fact of becoming a Christian often meant automatic exclusion from one's family, rejection by one's friends, and loss of all one's material possessions, social position, or political status.

What moved the first Christians to make such sacrifices and make them joyously was the gift they experienced of new life in

Christ—the gift of a transformation of attitudes and values, of a new way of looking at all things and evaluating them. The Christians knew that the grace of Jesus Christ had enlightened their minds and moved their hearts to understand and appreciate values they had never appreciated or even dreamed of before. This is what enabled them to live on a whole new plane of behavior. They experienced in their life the fruits of the Holy Spirit: joy, peace, and love above all, accompanied by patience, kindness, generosity, faith, mildness, and chaste self-control. (Gal. 5:22). They knew that something new, something wonderful and powerful had entered their lives, had happened to them as a result of their decision to accept the word of God and ask for the grace to be reborn as a member of the Body of Jesus Christ. The gift of the Holy Spirit was a tangible reality of their experience. The person of Jesus Christ was also an experienced reality to them: they knew that henceforth they had accepted Jesus, the incarnate Word of God, as the Way of life, the Truth of life, the very Life that gave meaning and ultimate value to the life they were born with.

In the light of this the early Christian saw serious sin—mortal sin—as a deep, deathly decision to abandon the way of Christ and return to the way of the world. One didn't pop in and out of accepting and rejecting Christ. The idea of being converted from sin, going back to it, turning back to Christ, returning again to sin, only to be converted again back to Christ was to the early Christian a contradiction in terms. And if we think a bit, we will realize that it is just as much a contradiction today, even to us. People do not pop in and out of mortal sin. If they are repeatedly commiting adultery, for example (which is certainly the serious matter required for mortal sin), then I think we should presume one of two things: either they are subjectively so unaware of the seriousness of what they are doing, or rendered so unfree by passion and deep, psychological needs that they are not subjectively guilty of committing mortal sin with sufficient knowledge and full consent of the will, or they are not truly repentant when they go to confession and, regardless of the absolution given by the priest, their sin is not forgiven.

It is not within our purpose—or our capability—to judge here which of these two alternatives is the more general reality in our day. We do not presume to judge (and no one can) whether such a person is committing mortal sin and not being absolved from it, or whether an individual in a particular case is, for subjective reasons, not personally guilty of mortal sin at all. The point we are making is one either is truly converted to Christ, truly renewed by his grace, or one is not. We are talking about basic life-options here; the fundamental disposition and orientation of one's life is something that does not easily change. No one accepts Jesus Christ as Lord and God one day and forgets all about Him to chase some passing creaturely gratification the next day in serious contradiction of the Gospel, and then turns painlessly back to Christ the next day by saying a few words in the confessional.

This is what the first Christians recognized very clearly. They knew more in this respect about human psychology than we do. If a person, after being converted to Christ, fell into serious, explicit sin, they did not presume it would be easy to really turn deeply back to Christ again. Either the sinner had not been converted very deeply and authentically the first time and thus the sinner's word was not to be taken very seriously, or else the sinner had been truly converted to Christ, had truly rejected Him, and really would not be converted back without some doing.

The first Christians emphasized reform of life, deep repentance of sin, and acts of penance as proof of the sincerity and strength of perseverance behind one's profession of conversion. The rite of sacramental Penance was for them the fire in which the gold is tested and purified. Absolution was preceded by long and public penance. And the man or woman who went through the rite of Penance and absolution knew he or she had been through something and had come out of it a different person.

All of this is a bit idealized, of course. Nothing in human life ever takes place exactly the way it is supposed to take place in theory. But the way the early Christians practiced confession shows, at least, how they thought of this sacrament and what they presumed it was supposed to accomplish.

What, by contrast, do we think of it? What do modern Catholics expect confession to accomplish in their lives?

What does Confession mean today?

WHAT DO CATHOLICS TODAY EXPECT confession to accomplish? I think that can be answered in one word: forgiveness. If Catholics today do something wrong, they want some assurance—some guarantee really—that God has forgiven them. Very often what they really want more than the assurance of God's forgiveness is the assurance that they are not going to go to hell for their sins. This might sound like the same thing, but it is not at all the same thing in the reality of the penitents' psychological and spiritual attitudes.

If I am going to confession out of fear, fear of otherwise being punished for my sins by some stern and vengeful God, then what really interests me in confession is not what effect my con-

fession has on me, but what effect it has on God. I am really not concerned very much about what kind of state I am in as a person (a husband, father, wife, mother, employer, employee, citizen, believer); what I want to know is what kind of state God is in. Is He angry with me? Is He going to throw me into hell if I die? I want to be in the state of grace because that is synonymous, in the context, with having a certified ticket good for one reserved seat in heaven. The state of grace is something God will honor and accept on judgment day.

Such an attitude toward God, toward sin, toward guilt, retribution, and placation of the deity presupposes and reveals an understanding of a human relationship to God that is certainly not Christian. It is vestigial paganism at best, and dangerously close to being actual, live paganism, not latent or vestigial at all, in spite of the fact that it is unrecognized. The attitude toward confession which we have described above differs very little, if at all, from the attitude with which a guilt-ridden native in the jungle would approach a witch doctor. Confession so understood and practiced is basically an act of magic; it is appreciated and engaged in as a guaranteed means of manipulating God. Absolution provides a talisman against the infinite unknown of the deity's power. It is not so much a human act that expresses and engages deeply the mind and heart of the penitent as it is a semi-magical act that changes the attitude of God.

It is my suggestion that this understanding of confession is encouraged, even inculcated, today by the way we practice private confession. In order that I might not be misunderstood, let me insist from the outset that I think private confession is potentially one of the most powerful, most helpful practices of the spiritual life. I am in favor of private confession—provided confession in private is used as it should be, with full awareness of what it is, what it is not, and what it must not be allowed to become. It must not be allowed to become just an easy out from guilt feelings in a person's life, a way to put off indefinitely the serious facing of what is keeping one from really living like a Christian.

So let us look at what private confession was in its beginnings. Private confession really began in the monasteries. It was a form of spiritual direction. It was used by monks whose whole life was bent on personal reform and growth in the life of grace. In confession a monk sought advice about his spiritual condition, and the priest imposed the kind of penance that would help him overcome whatever vices or deficiencies were blocking his spiritual progress. The penances were long and arduous, geared to reform of life.

But when this kind of confession was extended to the masses of the laity, which included a large percentage of people who did not even guess at what spiritual growth was all about, bare converts from paganism and their descendants—right down to the born Catholics, the cultural Christians of our own day—confession soon lost the character of spiritual direction and was reduced to a sin-shriving formality, at least for many people. Gradually the penances were reduced to a mere formality too—three Hail Mary's if you were good, a rosary or two if you were bad. And soon confession became what we know it to be today.

Even as such, confession remained a powerful sacrament for many, many persons, a fruitful medium of encounter with the living God. The grace of Christ works with power regardless of circumstances, and there is no question about the spiritual effectiveness of regular confession, even when the handicaps are heavy. But the fact remains that along with the working of the Holy Spirit in the heart during confession, along with the encounter with Jesus Christ embodied in and acting through the priest, along with the outpouring of the Father's love on every prodigal son who sought reconciliation through confession, there was present another reality: the implicit concept of confession as being just a process established for the removal of personal guilt in private. The very secrecy of the confessional encounter—a wise and merciful secrecy—reinforced the idea that confession was really a transaction between God and the individual soul, with the priest acting as God's personal representative, God's ear made available, God's forgiving voice made audible.

THE IDEA WAS OBSCURED AND ALL BUT LOST that confession is also a transaction between the individual penitent and the rest of the Christian community. The notion that individual Christians are accountable, must be accountable, to their fellow believers for the way they give public expression—or do not give public expression—to their faith was practically lost. The priest's role as judge, not only in the name of God, but also in the name of the community, was likewise lost. Priest and penitent alike tended more and more to reduce the priest's responsibility and function to that of speaking for God, and for God alone. Penitents were confessing their sins to God, through the medium of the priest; the priest was there to relay God's forgiveness to the penitents unless something was obviously deficient in the penitents' dispositions. The priest did not presume to ask many questions, or any questions at all, unless they were absolutely necessary. The whole idea was for the penitents to say to God what was burdening their souls, to get out whatever they had to say, and for this to be made as easy for them as possible. Penitents were not explaining themselves or accounting for their conduct to the Christian community or to the priest; they were simply mentioning all of their sins—and the emphasis was on getting them all mentioned, not leaving any out, getting them all out there on the counter—so that the priest, in the name of God, could wipe them all away. Any sin not mentioned was not wiped away (unless it was forgotten). If any unmentioned sin was remembered later, it had to be put onto the counter in a later confession. This self-revelation was presumed to be embarrassing and difficult (a presumption that was usually exaggerated or not warranted at all). For the priest to make it more embarrassing by asking questions was, in the language of pastoral theology, to make the sacrament odious, which was to be avoided at all costs. The idea was to make it easy for all of the people to get all of the sins out on the counter so that they could all be taken away and nothing would remain unconfessed to send a person to hell at the moment of death. Absolute secrecy was (and is) guaranteed so that no one would have any excuses or insurmountable difficulty to keep them from making an integral confession. To keep anything back in confession was about the worst thing a person could do.

It is enlightening to notice the role sexual sins began to play in this context. The whole aura of secrecy preconditioned the penitent to expect confession to be something embarrassing: the secret revelation in a dark closet of things experienced as shameful, things too embarrassing to talk about face to face. Children were assured that the priests would not even know who was talking to them, and in any case they could never reveal to anybody anything told them in confession. For most children, and most adults, about the only things they would want the assurance of secrecy for would be sexual sins and murder: sexual sins because of what the priest might think of them, murder because of what society might do to them if the truth leaked out. Since most people were not committing murder very often, this tended to give the confessional box the affective coloring of a secret little closet in which one whispered about sex or other things felt to be equally shameful. Even what was not shameful seemed to feel shameful in confession! It is perhaps significant, in confirmation of this, that just about the only sins that ever seemed to present any problem in terms of reform of life—any problem about receiving absolution or the validity of absolution given—were sins involving sex. Adolescents with habits of masturbation, married couples practicing birth control, someone involved in an illicit love affair tended to stay away from confession on the assumption that they could not have a sincere purpose of amendment. In some cases the priest might even have denied someone absolution for one of these things unless there was a promise to stop doing whatever one was doing. Other sins didn't have the same priority in confession as sexual sins. Sins not surrounded with any feeling of shamefulness didn't seem to count as much. People were rarely, if ever, denied absolution because of racial prejudice, for example. (One good reason for this was that people rarely, if ever, thought to mention racial prejudice as a sin). Business and politics hardly came up in confession. Perhaps these were considered ethical decisions rather than moral ones, just as the word immorality in popular language is spontaneously taken to refer to sexual misbehavior unless otherwise qualified. Whatever the reasons, sexual sins seemed to be the biggest thing one had to be worried about in confession, and about the only thing that might keep a person from absolution or communion if one did not reform. The insistence upon secrecy had a lot to do with this.

Private sin, public Confession and the Christian community

THE PRACTICE OF PRIVATE OR SECRET CONFESSION excluded the Christian community physically and visibly from the action that took place in confession. But in reality confession is not just a transaction between penitent and God with the priest in the middle. It is a transaction between an individual and God with the Christian community in the middle. It is to the church that the power to forgive sins is given. The only person who can exercise this power in virtue of his own office is the bishop, because the bishop is the official head of the local church. The bishop is the one who is officially empowered to speak for the Christian community in a given place. The bishop can forgive sins not only in the name of God but as the one who speaks in the name of the Christian community. In the name of the church the bishop receives back those who have separated themselves by sin from Christ and from the community of believers. Just as Baptism forgives sin by incorporating a person into Christ who died on the cross in expiation of sin and rose again in newness of life, and just as we are incorporated into Christ through being visibly incorporated into his visible Body on earth, the church, so confession forgives sin by being a visible re-incorporation, a re-integration, into the Christian assembly. It is not that we totally cease to be members of the Body of Christ through sin, but if our sin is serious, is mortal, we cease to be live members, members in full, vital contact with other members and with the Head of the Body, who is Christ. Every mortal sin is an act of separating oneself from the life of the church. It is an act of leaving the church in a very real way. In a sense that is more truth than exaggeration. Every mortal sin is a denial of the faith. We do not by every sin formally renounce our belief. But we do break with our fellow believers. In action we deny the faith. By freely choosing to act in a way incompatible with the teaching of Jesus Christ, we implicitly deny that we really believe in his teaching in any real, self-engaging way. We cease to stand together with our fellow Christians in affirmation of the world-view of Jesus Christ.

The first real consciousness the church came to regarding the power to forgive sin after Baptism occurred during the time of persecution. Some Christians under torture or fear of death denied Christ. They were released from prison. When they tried to return to the Christian assembly to celebrate the Eucharist, they were received with startled, puzzled looks which asked: "What are you doing here? You do not believe in Christ." In vain did the released prisoners protest that they really did believe in Christ, that they had just denied Him out of weakness and fear under threat of death. The early Christians were so conscious of the Gospel's demand that one be willing to lose one's life in order to save it, so convinced of the power of grace, of the new life of Christ and the gifts of the Holy Spirit in the hearts of those who believe, that they simply could not understand how anyone reborn in Christ, truly converted to Him, could deny Him one day and reaffirm belief in Him the next. You can die and be brought back to life once; but you can't go about dying and being reborn again every other week. So the released Christian prisoners had to convince not only God, but their fellow believers that their conversion back to Christ was sincere. And this, as we have seen, required some doing. It required years, sometimes a lifetime, of hard, public penance.

In this process the person who spoke in the name of the Christian community was the bishop. It was the bishop who listened to the story, weighed the penitent's sincerity, decided what penance should be imposed to test and strengthen the conversion back to Christ, and finally received the penitent back into the Christian community, back into full participation in the sacramental, Eucharistic life of the church. The absolution (which only the bishop gave) was just as visibly an act of re-incorporation into the church, of reintegration into the community, as it was an act of removing sins. The absolution, like the penance and the confession itself, took place in public, in the midst of the whole Christian assembly.

THIS HISTORICAL SKETCH is greatly simplified, but in broad, general lines, it paints the historical origin of sacramental confession. What the history brings out is the authentic nature of confession as a very communitarian act. Before the penitents received absolution, before they were accepted back into full membership in the community, they satisfied the whole community about the depth and sincerity of their conversion to Jesus Christ. The bishop questioned them in the name of the community, imposed penances that would make their conversion credible to the community, and received them back in the name of the community. There was nothing private, and nothing secret about it.

Later and very gradually over a period of centuries Christians became conscious of more and more actions that were, in themselves, incompatible with profession of the Christian faith. Adultery and murder were ranged alongside of apostasy as acts that placed a person outside of the Christian community, in a stance of separation from the living Body of Christ. As time passed, the Christian people came to realize that any really deliberate free decision to act against the teaching of Christ in a serious matter is a decision, for the time being at least, to break with Christ and with his people, an implicit denial of the faith, a rupture of the bonds of communal hope and love. The need for confession and sacramental absolution was extended to every mortal sin. And mortal covered a multitude of sins.

Since so many of the sins recognized as mortal were private, and since public confession of them could do untold harm in many cases, the practice of private, secret confession grew up. As we have seen, in this practice the true nature of confession as a communal act and the nature of absolution as an act in the name of the Christian community were obscured. The bishop delegated to priests his authority to absolve and to speak in the name of the community in reconciliation of sinners. This too obscured the nature of confession and absolution as a transaction between the individual penitent and the whole community of the church.

Confession no longer appeared as a visible, public profession of conversion away from sins the whole community was aware of. It was simply a private removal of personal, secret guilt. Less and less did the priest question, impose penance, and judge the sincerity of one's conversion in the name of the community, requiring evidence of conversion that was credible to human eyes. He just absolved in the name of the God who reads the heart, warning the penitent that any insincerity would be known to God, and that God could not be mocked.

Such a warning might be adequate in the case of conscious, deliberate insincerity. But most of us sinners are good at bamboozling ourselves. Our deception of others is no greater than the unconscious, unrecognized deception we practice on ourselves. We rationalize, we shade things, we stick to a pretty vague and general level of accusation even in our own examinations of conscience. Anyone who has talked to prisoners in a jail, or alcoholics in a ward can tell you the difference between the way an offender sees himself and the way his case stands up in court in the light of objective questioning and evidence.

What are we to say? That private confession should be abolished? God preserve us from that. That rigorous, public penance should be reinstated? May God have mercy on us! But that something should be done to make confession less of an individual, private affair between a sinner and God, with the priest a rather passive middleman in between, yes, by all means.

What can be done to make Confession work?

WE MUST FIND A WAY to give the Christian community a voice in the judgment of an individual penitent's sin. And we must find a way to give the Christian community some assurance of the sincerity and depth of each individual penitent's conversion. If a man's real sin is drinking to such an extent that no authentic Christian family life is possible in his home, then that man should not be able to receive the assurance of reconciliation with the Christian community from a priest until his wife has been heard about his case, and his wife and children have seen a radical reform in his behavior. If a woman's prejudice in the area of race relations is making Christian community impossible or very difficult in her parish, then that woman should not be able to receive sacramental assurance of her good standing with God in the church until she has changed her attitude and her behavior in a way that publicly repairs the scandal she has been to the community of faith. It should not be left only to the individual to be the accuser in confession. The community should have something to say about whether a person is living in a way that expresses the authentic Gospel of Jesus Christ.

I don't mean that the community should be the ultimate judge as if some kind of ecclesiastical People's Court should be set up. The bishop (or his delegate the priest) is the only one who can judge sin in the name of the church or can decide whether absolution should be given. But the priest should not have to make that judgment—in every case at least—without any evidence being admitted from any person other than the penitent. In other words, we must make confession an act of accountability to the Christian community as well as to the priest and God.

How can this be done? How can it not be done? I think we must exclude any solution that simply scratches out the centuries of Christian experience within which our present confessional practice evolved. There is no question of abolishing private confession, of allowing the sacramental seal of secrecy to be violated in any manner or degree. We do not want to get into public confession of private sins or to impose crushing burdens of penance upon people. These are all lessons that history has taught us.

What, then, can we do?

First, let us recognize that very few of the sins confessed to a priest are actually secret. Most of them are very well known to everyone who lives with, works with, or in any way interacts with the penitent enough to know the penitent as a person. Many more sins are known to at least one other person. Perhaps we should each adopt a policy of not bringing our sins to the priest in confession until some kind of public confession and reparation has been made to those who have seen and suffered from those sins. Other persons should have an opportunity to speak if necessary or helpful. The sins we commit in our home should be faced as sin in the presence of our family, at least of the adult members, according to circumstances, and there should be some agreement on what a truly Christian reform of life means for us. This principle can be applied, due adjustments being made, to each level of Christian community of which a person is a part.

Second, when we examine our consciences we should all take as a guiding assumption that very few people confess their real sins and that it is not very likely that we, without any help from others, are going to be exceptions. This can sound like cynicism, but I believe the overall fruits of sacramental confession in the church are enough to bear out the assumption. The sins that destroy individual, family, or social life are not the sins that we easily face in ourselves or bring up in confession. If we are aware of this, we will not be content just to confess individual acts of sin. These are more likely to be symptoms than our real disease, as Father Tad Guzie explains in *Confession for Today's Catholic* (Claretian Publications, 1976). What we confess as sin is usually the fruit of our real sin. And it is our real sin—some deep, willful attitude or accepted value in the core of our heart that is contrary to the values of Christ—that we want to repent for and bring to confession.

If we have been confessing that we drink too much, for example, we should ask ourselves just what that too much refers to in our minds, and how much drinking we are accustomed to accept as not being too much. It may be we should not presume to

bring our drinking to the priest in confession until we have sat down with husband or wife (or friends or employer) and discussed just what effect they think our drinking is having on our family life, business life, and social relationships. We should listen to what they think we ought to do about it.

The same policy will apply to most other sins; to all in fact except those which are really so secret that others do not know they are going on. And these types are rare. If there is adultery for example that is not known to one's spouse, it probably should not be made known to the spouse. But it should be discussed with someone who can help us get to causes and remedies. It may be we should consult a competent marriage counselor who appreciates the value of Christian marriage before we ask absolution from the church. If the adultery is known to both parties of the marriage, then perhaps husband and wife should go to a marriage counselor together, looking for the faults on both sides that led to the infidelity, and not presuming too quickly that it was just a simple, momentary lapse of virtue.

In all of this our goal should be to find the real sins that are destroying us, our family life, or the society of which we are a part.

Third, we should understand very clearly that the penance imposed by the priest and accepted by us is supposed to be something that will both express and foster a real reform of life in the area of the sins confessed. We should not settle for a token penance if the priest gives us one (like "three Hail Mary's and three Our Father's"). If the penance given won't work and we know it won't, we should say so. If necessary we should come prepared to suggest our own.

If we have a drinking problem, we should not consider ourselves fully reconciled with the church until we have, in penance, changed our drinking habits for a long enough time to give some assurance of permanence. Our penance might be to consult a professional about problem drinking, or to give up the crutch of alcohol altogether for five years, until we have learned what life can be like without it.

If we are chronically boring or boorish to our spouse, we should not consider our reception of the sacrament of reconciliation complete until we have learned to talk in a way that includes listening, thinking, and sensitivity. Our penance might be to make a Marriage Encounter or to read a book on fighting fair in marriage or even to take a course in Transactional Analysis. The penance should be more than a gesture; it should be an effective means to clear up the cause of our difficulty.

It is the sin at the root of our sins—the sin seldom confessed and even more seldom remedied—that breaks up marriages and renders family life destructive to children. And so we should call the source of evil in our life by its right name: it is sin. When love, joy, and peace do not characterize our life, the explanation is not just some given fact, like lack of communication, or deep, personal insecurity, or tension and dissatisfaction. The real explanation is the free, deliberate sin of not doing anything about such a lack. Lack of communication, insecurity, and tension are conscience matters, not because they exist, but because we are not taking adequate measures to deal with them. And when we bring our sins to confession, the penance we receive should be a lever that works us out of the deep-worn ruts of the sin that is most characteristic and lethal in our lives.

In some cases the penance might follow absolution as is our present practice. In other cases absolution might be deferred until we have given external evidence of a sincere intention to reform our life. Or absolution might be given with the stipulation that we return to confession at stated intervals until both we and the confessor are satisfied that our conversion is a sincere and stable one. There is nothing wrong with our suggesting such a procedure to the priest. After all, in this the priest is like a doctor who can't know whether or not the medicines are working unless we speak up about whether or not we are cured.

We should be very conscious here that a truly effective penance may have to include a way to open up a whole new dimension of prayer in our lives. It may well be that a given person (I believe it is true for most persons) will not find it even remotely possible to begin leading a truly Christian life, or to build a truly Christian marriage, unless he or she takes up prayer in a serious and regular way. Doctors do not hesitate to insist that heart patients spend anywhere from half an hour to an hour or more in physical exercise—under pain of death. We should encourage our confessors not to hesitate to require as much prayer as is necessary to bring us up to the level of the actual challenge in our life. The measure of prayer demanded by the Gospel of Jesus Christ—demanded under pain of spiritual death—is whatever measure necessary for a given person to live up to the Christian responsibilities of a given state of life: "Pray that you enter not into temptation." Pray until you are able to overcome temptation. We were taught as children to confess it if we did not say our morning and night prayers. But morning and night prayers are not in themselves either necessary or sufficient.

How much we must pray as Christians is determined by how much we need to pray in order to live as a Christian in all the areas of life. If at certain periods of life we need to invest an hour or even more than an hour a day in prayer in order to be equal to the temptations and challenges we face as Christians, then that is how much time we are obliged to pray—under pain of spiritual death. And it is our duty to face our actual situation as Christians and to make whatever decisions are necessary to live a full and authentic Christian life.

Fourth, we should take a new look at the assumptions we Christians bring to an examination of conscience. Do we examine our consciences for sins—understanding by this word actions that are bad? Or do we examine our consciences to see whether we are bearing the fruits of a Christian life? It is significant that in the best-known gospel description of the General Judgment, nobody who goes to hell is sent there for a mortal sin! "I was hungry and you did not give me to eat; thirsty and you did not give me to drink; naked and you did not clothe me; sick and in prison and you did not visit me." (Mt. 25:42-46). If you consult the books of moral theology, you will find that it is all but impossible, according to the morality we have been taught, for a Christian in normal circumstances to commit a mortal sin of not feeding the hungry, clothing the naked, or visiting the sick and imprisoned. And yet Jesus uses precisely these examples as the criteria for eternal salvation or damnation in his description of the Judgment. Perhaps we should take another look at the morality we were taught.

Finding a way to change your life

IF WE LOOK CLOSELY INTO THE SCRIPTURES we will find that Jesus himself constantly bases his judgment of a person's life, not on the sins committed, but on the fruits grace has borne in that life. "Every branch in me that does not bear fruit will be cut off and cast into the fire" (John 15:2). The man who received only one talent and did not invest it, but buried it in the ground until his master's return was condemned. And yet he did nothing bad with the talent that was entrusted to him. He did not lose it. He gave it back intact. And so with our lives: If we do nothing bad with them and nothing good, we deserve to be condemned.

If we simply preserve the state of grace in ourselves, guarding it like pickles in a jar, but do not let the grace that has been given us act and bear fruit in the world, we stand condemned.

We are to be the salt of the earth, the light of the world, the leaven in the dough. If Christians do not act and if the bread of the world does not rise, then the Gospel tells us those inactive Christians will be cast out as unfaithful stewards of the riches entrusted to them. The salt that gives no flavor to the world is good for nothing but to be cast out and tramped on. The man and woman whose faith and love for God do not inflame the hearts of their own children, for example, have something to examine their consciences about.

We are familiar with these themes from Scripture. But they do not constitute the basis of our judgment on our lives. Because they are not the basis on which we examine our consciences before confession, there is something seriously wrong. Scripture tells us that at death Christ will judge us on how much fruit grace has borne in our lives. But we prepare for the judgment of the priest in confession—which is supposed to be a preview and a preparation for the final examen at death—by examining ourselves according to an entirely different standard. We judge ourselves on how much bad we have done. Jesus is going to judge us on how much good we have done. With this kind of mix-up taking place, we might have to expect a lot of surprises on Judgment Day. And the sobering truth is that this is exactly what Jesus has warned us to expect: "Lord, when did I see you hungry, or thirsty, or naked?" In the scenes of judgment—the separation of the sheep and the goats, the condemnation of the man who buried his talent in the ground—those condemned are surprised at their condemnation. They were preparing for judgment according to one standard, but they were actually going to be judged according to another standard. No one can rightfully plead ignorance of this, because Jesus has made it perfectly plain in the Gospel what the judgment is going to be about. But it is just as plain that we are paying no attention to the warning He gives. And He knew we wouldn't. That is why He keeps trying so hard to keep warning us through the words of his Gospel.

We are accustomed to examine our conscience before confession according to lists drawn up by moral theologians and devotional writers. We were given the impression that if it isn't on the list, it isn't a sin. And so sins like a willful ignorance of the church's teaching since Vatican II, a rejection of the new liturgy, racial segregation in our cities and schools (public and private), overcrowding of prisoners in county jails and state-owned (that is, citizen-owned) prisons, political Cainism ("Am I my brother's keeper?"), superficial communication between spouses, lack of communication between parents and children, failure to seek and accept psychological counseling when necessary, material cooperation in immoral business and political activities, failure to call elected representatives to account for their stewardship, neglect of one's elderly parents or grandparents, unsafe driving habits, consumer patronage of unworthy products—these and most of the other sins, personal as well as social, that are actually undermining the foundations of the Kingdom of God all remain unrecognized, unrepented, unconfessed, and unreconciled in this life, whether or not we have grounds to hope they will be forgiven in the next.

We MUST CULTIVATE WITHIN OURSELVES a new consciousness that what the Gospel means in calling for reform of life is not a stricter observance of the Ten Commandments. The Gospel calls for a whole restructuring of one's life according to a radically new set of attitudes and values. Those attitudes and values are just as much news today as they were in the first days when the Christian preaching was known as the good news. And the people who live by them will find today, just as in the time of the Apostles, that any life embodying the good news of Christ will be bad news for the surrounding world. Persecution is not just a possibility for the fervent Christian; it is a promise. In other words, Christian men and women must be very conscious that the kind of morality to which a Christian is obliged is not the going morality of the surrounding culture, no matter how good that culture is. If Christians are not bearing prophetic witness to values that are in advance of the cultural values of their milieu, those Christians are not living an authentic Christian life. They have not reformed their lives according to the Gospel and they have some repenting, some changing of their minds to do.

The temptation to be concrete with examples is a pressing one here. But any example one can offer that is worth anything will be, by definition, so contrary to what people are accustomed to think and accept that each example would require a whole chapter of qualifications, answers to objections, and justification. Nevertheless, I offer the following suggestions as

nothing but leading questions for further prayer and reflection.
Jesus says that we should turn the other cheek, go a second
mile with the man who forces us to walk one, and hand over our

coat as well to the person who sues us for our shirt (Matt. 5:39ff.). If these words are not rules (and they aren't), then they must be examples intended to teach us the way Jesus evaluates persons and things. Have we understood what He is trying to say, and if so, can we point to any concrete effects this is having on our lives?

The principle behind these examples is just that we should never lose our relationship with any human because of hurt feelings, the value we place on our time, or the loss of any material thing. People are more important than things. Friendship mustn't withdraw in the face of rejection. Love takes priority over getting things done.

T O MAKE RULES OUT OF WHAT was just said is to invite the unrealistic. But to make a guiding principle out of these values is to make Christ's mind our own, and to have a very practical norm by which to judge our day-to-day conduct. How many times have we argued or fallen out with others over nothing but material things, burdens placed on our time, or hurt caused to our feelings? Sometimes one has to protest, of course; but when were our objections based on true conflicting obligations and values, and when did they just come from a false, more selfish set of priorities? How many relatives don't speak to each other any more because of quarrels over money? How many fights in the home come from the way one person treats or mistreats another's things? How many friendships have died because someone was not able to expose the other cheek by coming back after an experience of hurt, misunderstanding, or rejection?

Here is another example. Jesus taught, "None of you can be my disciple if he does not renounce all his possessions" (Luke 14:33), and "No man can serve two masters . . . You cannot give yourself to God and money" (Luke 16:13). Then He told the story of the rich man (Dives) who went to hell because of his attitude toward the poor man (Lazarus) who lay at his doorstep.

What does this teaching mean? Obviously we don't have to give away all our possessions in fact, but what does it mean to really renounce them from the heart? What signs are there in our lives, in our homes, that we really do not cling to any material thing? What do we do that expresses this? Do we serve money as a master? How often do we feel we have to have something just because it is advertised, popular, convenient, or a status symbol? How often is our Christian idealism made uncomfortable by the policies of the establishment we work for? How often do we, as consumers, feel we are voting with our dollar bill for junk? How often does our buying support economic practices we consider immoral and destructive of human society? What god are we serving in some of the ways we work and buy and sell? Have we capitulated to the economic system as to our master, a god too powerful and too dangerous to challenge? And who is Lazarus in our day? Where is our doorstep in this age of jets and telstar?

We could ask ourselves and one another some very practical questions: "Why did I really buy that particular product? Why in that particular store? What business policy is my money supporting? What alternatives were, or are, available? Are there alternatives that should be available and are not? Why not?"

Ask those questions about the last jar of peanut butter you bought. About the last loaf of bread.

Look together at the family budget. How much goes for what? How much goes to sharing with the poor?

A final example: The Apostles teach that Christian women should not braid their hair, wear gold ornaments or expensive clothing (1 Peter 3; 1 Tim 2). These were obviously cultural symbols in their day; so much so that recent editions of the Bible translate braided hair as elaborate hairstyles. So we do not take these instructions as rules for our time.

But we have to look for, and respect, the principle behind them. What were the Apostles really getting at? Let us not talk about immodesty in dress, since that just invites argument and ridicule. Let us ask instead what our dress—for men and women—expresses. What image of yourself are you trying to project through your choice of clothes? What value system are you accepting—and voting for with your money—if you decide to follow a particular style? What set of values do you think inspired the people who designed this style? Do your friends, your dates, your family agree that your clothes do express, objectively, the image of yourself that you intend them to express?

The examination I have proposed is a modest beginning compared to the vast moral problems confronting the Christian conscience today. But if we start with what is easy and near at hand, we may gradually find the courage to deal with the problem of our cooperation as citizens in such sins as the oppression of minorities, illegitimate support of dictatorial foreign governments, military aid to police states that use torture as a matter of policy, the bribery of presidents by our highest-ranking business leaders, the diffusion of pornography, sexual promiscuity, multiplying abortions, industrial pollution, and ecological devastation.

The really important thing is to begin. We have to recognize that sin is an active force in the world which can be overcome only by the grace of the Gospel of Jesus Christ lived out in its entirety. And I believe we are failing as a Christian people to live the Gospel in a way that brings the redemption of Christ to the world. How else explain the fact that millions of Christians who receive Holy Communion every Sunday are having so little impact on society? How could Adolf Hitler use all the resources of a Christian Germany to invade Europe and cremate six million Jews? How can the military junta in Chile, a Catholic country, continue to reign by torture and terrorism while the hierarchy protests in vain? How can church-going America be so permeated with materialism and responsible for so much of the materialism that other nations have succumbed to in imitation of us? If we are a Christian people, how explain the fact that in our nation's capital in 1975 there were more legal abortions recorded than live births? Finally, why do so many faithfully practicing Catholic parents see their children leave the church just as soon as they are able to make the decision for themselves?

Our Lord said, "By their fruits you shall know them." I think it is time we thought about the corollary: "By our fruits we must judge ourselves."